Off the Wall

HOCKNEY POSTERS

Off the Wall

HOCKNEY POSTERS

PAVILION

HOCKNEY

First published in Great Britain in 1994 by

PAVILION BOOKS LIMITED

26 Upper Ground, London SE1 9PD

Posters © *David Hockney* 1994

Foreword © *Brian Baggott* 1994

Designed by *Peter Bridgewater*

Typeset in *Monotype Janson and Helvetica*

A CIP catalogue record for this book is available
from the British Library

ISBN 1 85793 421 0

Printed and bound in Italy by New Interlitho

2 4 6 8 10 9 7 5 3 1

This book may be ordered by post direct from the publisher.
Please contact the Marketing Department.
But try your bookshop first

ACKNOWLEDGEMENTS

Acknowledgements and thanks must go to members of Mr Hockney's staff: Karen
Kuhlman, Lisa McPherson and Richard Schmidt in Los Angeles and Cavan Butler
in England. Also Jonathan Silver and his assistants at 1853 Gallery, Salts Mill,
Bradford, Catherine Barry and Colin Webb at Pavilion Books, and all the kind
people too numerous to mention at art galleries worldwide.
I also wish to express my gratitude and thanks to Rodney Jonas, Francisco Carnato,
Garry Carr and Keith Bolt for their unstinting assistance at all times.
Finally, David Hockney himself for his unfailing energy and generosity.

HOCKNEY

In 1987, Pavilion Books published *Hockney Posters*, a selection of some of the finest examples of David Hockney's work in this medium, based on my own collection of posters. *Off the Wall* follows up the success of the first book, with examples of Mr Hockney's work from 1987 right up to 1994, which includes some of his most innovative and vibrant work.

I have been collecting posters since the mid-1970s, having realized that this was a means of owning an exciting and significant body of work at an affordable price. I have been encouraged in my collecting by David Hockney's revived interest in poster design in recent years. His interest forms part of a general move towards working with new media – photo-collages, faxes, Xerox machines – popular and accessible means of reproducing art. Providing that they are quality reproductions, he proves that posters are worth keeping as works of art and can be as collectable as oil paintings.

My collection is virtually definitive, but with qualifications – often several similar images have been created for different exhibitions, some of which have not been reproduced here. For us the term 'Hockney poster' is a fairly loose concept, which we take to mean any poster that contains an image made by David Hockney, and not necessarily one where the artist has also produced the graphics. For instance, the poster *Dash*, number 89 in the index, was designed by Adrian Gray, using a David Hockney image.

This new book selects 38 of Hockney's most recent posters reproduced in large format, which reflect his wide influence and international appeal. The pictorial index at the back of the book places these new posters in their chronological context. They are ordered by the year that the image was created, and within that year, in order of the date of the exhibition. Thus an early image such as *Doll Boy*, created in 1961, is the first poster in the index, despite the fact that it was not used in a poster until 1991. This also highlights the contemporary feel of Hockney's early images which still have currency today.

Brian Baggott, 1994

Die Ausstellung findet
mit Unterstützung
des British Council statt.

David Hockney »Doll Boy«, 1960/61

HAMBURGER KUNSTHALLE

Hamburger Kunsthalle
Glockengießerwall

6. November 1991
bis 12. Januar 1992
tägl. außer montags
10 bis 18 Uhr

Im Blickfeld

David Hockney
»Doll Boy«

Die Kunsthalle
ist am 24.12.
und am 31.12.
geschlossen,

am 1.1.1992 ist von
12 bis 18 Uhr geöffnet.

David Hockney

Seven Paintings

18 February – 26 July 1992

New Displays 1992
sponsored by
British Petroleum

Admission free
Broadsheet £1.50
Monday–Saturday 10–5.50
Sunday 2–5.50
Closed 17 April, 4 May
Pimlico Underground
Recorded Information
071-821 7128

TATE
GALLERY

paintings drawings and prints from private collections

DAVID HOCKNEY

A PRIVATE VIEW

OCTOBER 26 TO NOVEMBER 12 1988 MONDAY TO FRIDAY 10 TO 6 SATURDAY 10 TO 2 AT EDITIONS GRAPHIQUES GALLERY

3 CLIFFORD STREET NEW BOND STREET LONDON W1X 1RA

DAVID HOCKNEY: A RETROSPECTIVE THE METROPOLITAN MUSEUM OF ART
JUNE 18 - AUGUST 14, 1988

The exhibition is made possible by AT&T.

This exhibition was organized by the Los Angeles County Museum of Art and is supported by an indemnity from the Federal Council on the Arts and the Humanities.

DAVID HOCKNEY

A RETROSPECTIVE

FEBRUARY 4 – APRIL 24, 1988

LOS ANGELES COUNTY MUSEUM OF ART

La Virreina : **exposicions**

Palau de la Virreina
Espai 2
La Rambla, 99
08002 Barcelona
Tel. 301 77 75

DAVID HOCKNEY

Dues cadires de platja. Calvi 1972

Del 12 de gener al 28 de febrer de 1993

Fundación Juan March

Ajuntament de Barcelona
Àrea de Cultura

DAVID HOCKNEY

HAWAII OPERA THEATRE

Twenty-sixth season 1986   The Tales of Hoffmann   The Rake's Progress   Tosca

Kerby (After Hogarth) Useful Knowledge.   © David Hockney 1975

The Lady and the Clarinet
A New Comedy by Michael Cristofer

MARK TAPER FORUM. AUG 14 - SEPT 28.
GORDON DAVIDSON, ARTISTIC DIRECTOR ● CENTER THEATRE GROUP. MUSIC CENTER.

WORLD PREMIERE
First Production of the 1980-81 Season.

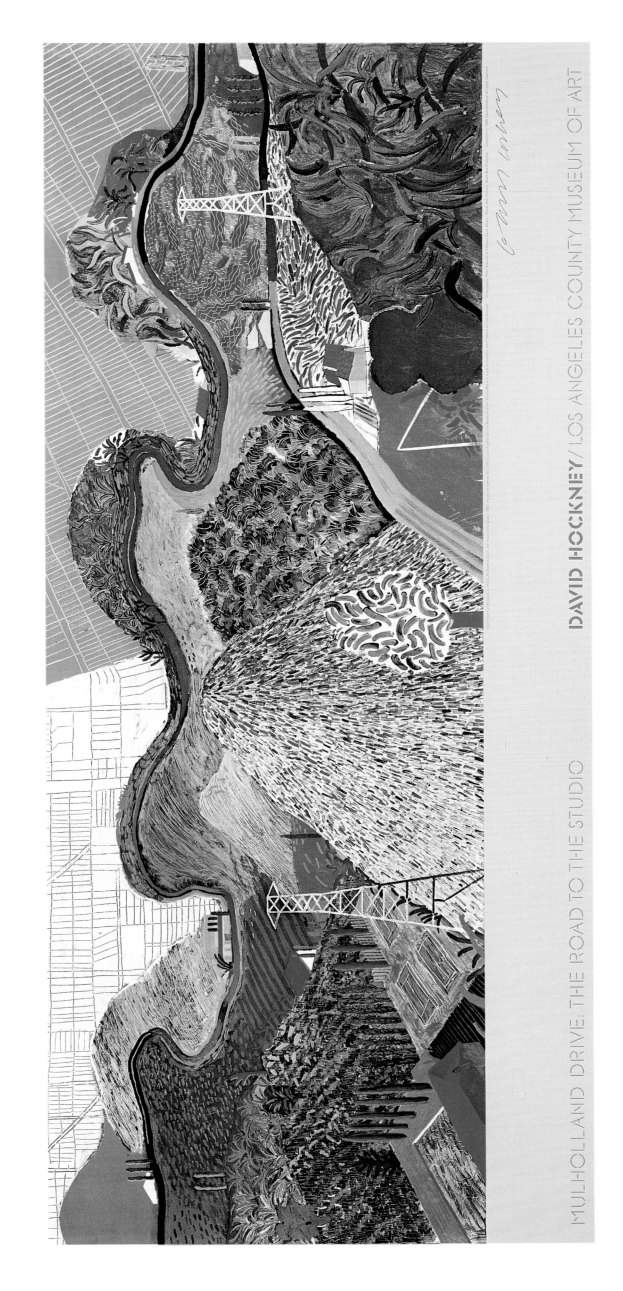

DAVID HOCKNEY/LOS ANGELES COUNTY MUSEUM OF ART

MULHOLLAND DRIVE: THE ROAD TO THE STUDIO

DAVID HOCKNEY: A RETROSPECTIVE THE METROPOLITAN MUSEUM OF ART

JUNE 18 – AUGUST 14, 1988

DAVID HOCKNEY: A RETROSPECTIVE
THE METROPOLITAN MUSEUM OF ART

JUNE 18 - AUGUST 14, 1988

The exhibition is made possible by AT&T.

This exhibition was organized by the Los Angeles County Museum of Art and is supported by an indemnity from the Federal Council on the Arts and the Humanities.

DAVID HOCKNEY

L'Enfant et les sortileges.

The Contemporary Museum, Honolulu, Hawaii

Acrylic on canvas and wood, carpeting, wool, velour, laminated foam board and colored light   Overall diameter 132" × 288" × 432"   © David Hockney, 1983

DAVID HOCKNEY

Graphics and Photocollages 1965-88

Art Gallery ARTIUM Opening Event

©DAVID HOCKNEY／"Views of Hotel Well III"1985, Lithograph.

デイヴィッド・ホックニー版画回顧展 1965-88
──ハリウッドコレクションからツリーまで──
会期＝1989年4月12日(水)～5月14日(日)
10:00AM～8:00PM
会場＝三菱地所アルティアム／福岡市中央区天神1-7-11 イムズ8F TEL.092-733-2001
主催＝三菱地所アルティアム、西日本新聞社
後援＝ブリティッシュ・カウンシル、福岡県教育委員会、福岡市教育委員会、NHK福岡放送局、テレビ西日本 協力＝APS
入場料＝一般 500(400)円、大学・高校生 400(300)円、中学生 300(200)円、小学生以下無料
(　)内は前売、20名以上の団体料金です。

ART GALLERY
ARTIUM

PRESENTED BY MITSUBISHI-JISHO

DAVID HOCKNEY

DAVID HOCKNEY

Prints from Tyler Graphics 1984–1986

Thordén Wetterling Galleries, Gothenburg, March 3–April 6

The Chair, 1985   *Oil on Canvas, 48" x 36"*

DAVID   HOCKNEY

at the Junior Arts Center, Cotsen Fellow 1988
Barnsdall Art Park, Los Angeles

The Cotsen Artist Award is a memorial to JoAnne Stolaroff Cotsen and her love of children and art. It provides funds to bring an internationally renowned artist to the Junior Arts Center for a day in-residence with young art students from the community.

The Junior Arts Center is a division of the City of Los Angeles Cultural Affairs Department, Tom Bradley, Mayor; Rodney Punt, General Manager.   Published by Heritage Artwork (213) 856-8920   Photo by Steve Oliver   ©David Hockney, 1985

S A N   F R A N C I S C O
GIRLS CHORUS

ELIZABETH APPLING · ARTISTIC DIRECTOR

1 9 8 8 – 1 9 8 9

T E N T H   A N N I V E R S A R Y

Festival Season

DAVID HOCKNEY "THE RED POT, APRIL, 1986" HOMEMADE PRINT 14" × 8½". PHOTO: RICHARD SCHMIDT © DAVID HOCKNEY

for Brian
love David

Art for Equality

At the **ICA Nash Rooms** London SW1 from **9th to 13th April 1991** A benefit for the **Iris Trust** organised by the **Stonewall Group**

Red Flowers and Blue Spots 1986 Acrylic on Canvas
copyright **David Hockney** 1986

ホックニーのオペラ展
HOCKNEY'S OPERA

DAVID HOCKNEY
TRISTAN AND ISOLDE
Model for Act. 1

1986/87
gouache, acrylic, foam core, plexiglas, photocopy prints, velvet paper and wood
5in.×9in.×6½in.

Illustration © David Hockney

DAVID HOCKNEY

A RETROSPECTIVE

FEBRUARY 4 - APRIL 24. 1988

LOS ANGELES COUNTY MUSEUM OF ART

DAVID HOCKNEY: A RETROSPECTIVE
THE METROPOLITAN MUSEUM OF ART

JUNE 18 - AUGUST 14, 1988   The exhibition is made possible by AT&T.

This exhibition was organized by the Los Angeles County Museum of Art and is supported by an indemnity from the Federal Council on the Arts and the Humanities.

STILL LIFE WITH FLOWERS. Acrylic on canvas, 1987. David Hockney (born 1937) British. Courtesy of the artist. Reproduced by permission © David Hockney 1987 © 1988 The Metropolitan Museum of Art   02-02538-5 AA

TATE GALLERY
DAVID HOCKNEY

David Hockney b.1937   'My Mother Bridlington 1988' 1988 © the artist   Designed by David Hockney   Published by Tate Gallery Publications, Millbank, London SW1P 4RG   Printed in Great Britain by Westerham Press Ltd., Westerham, Kent

NOW ART CAN PROLONG LIFE AS WELL AS IMITATE IT.

"Bowl of Fruit & Spotted Floor," 1988, oil on canvas, 24 x 24 in.,
©David Hockney, 1988

ART
AGAINST
AIDS
LOS ANGELES

Original Logo Designed by Dan Friedman

ART EXHIBITION AND SALE
PACIFIC DESIGN CENTER/MURRAY FELDMAN GALLERY
DECEMBER 15, 1988 THRU FEBRUARY 5, 1989
VIEWING HOURS: TUESDAY THRU FRIDAY 11:00-6:00
SATURDAY & SUNDAY 12:00-6:00

Printed by Dual Graphics/Don Marquis/TH Graphics
Poster Designed by Gallison Pearman/Los Angeles
Photography: Richard Schmidt
Art Against AIDS Los Angeles is a joint venture of AIDS Project
Los Angeles and the American Foundation for AIDS Research.

DAVID HOCKNEY

PUBLISHED EXCLUSIVELY BY MIRAGE EDITIONS, INC. IN ASSOCIATION WITH THE WEST HOLLYWOOD MARKETING CORPORATION

Die Frau ohne Schatten

RICHARD STRAUSS

ROYAL OPERA HOUSE
Covent Garden

TIVOLI 1993/David Hockney: "The Twenty Fourth V.N. Painting" 1992 (Detail)/Oil on Canvas/© David Hockney

William Hardie Gallery

in association with Murray Johnstone Ltd

The Eleventh V.N. Painting

DAVID HOCKNEY
Some Very New Paintings

28 June - 27 August 1993
Mon - Fri: 10 - 5pm   Sat: 10 - 1pm

141 West Regent Street Glasgow. Tel: 041-221 6780

some local
snaps
by
David Hockney

A
LOCAL
ARTIST

made in June 1993 with
a pocket 35mm camera
and enlarged and
printed by laser
machine including a
Jumbo picture of Coxwold
for
1853 Gallery Salts Mill

1 DAVID HOCKNEY: DOLL BOY

Im Blickfeld Hamburger Kunsthalle, 1991
33 x 20 in; 84 x 53 cm
Doll Boy, 1960

2 DAVID HOCKNEY: WE TWO

BOYS TOGETHER CLINGING

Spotlight, National Touring Exhibition, Arts
Council Collection, 1994
11 x 8 in; 29.7 x 21.3 cm
We Two Boys Together Clinging, 1961

3 TOWARDS ART?

Victoria Street Gallery, Nottingham, 1963
30 x 20 in; 76.5 x 51 cm
Image also used: Laing Art Gallery
Towards Art?, 1962

4 LOOK AT HOCKNEY

Galerie Thomas, Düsseldorf, 1970
37 x 27 in; 94 x 69.9 cm
The Marriage, 1962

5 150 ANNIVERSARY EXHIBITION

Printmaking from the Royal College of Art, 1987
Barbican Centre
30 x 20 in; 76 x 51.9 cm
The Diploma, 1962

6 A RAKE'S PROGRESS AND OTHER

ETCHINGS BY DAVID HOCKNEY

Editions Alecto, 1963
34¼ x 22½ in; 87 x 57 cm
A Rake's Progress, 1963

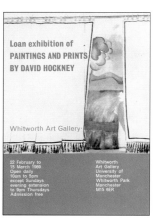

7 LOAN EXHIBITION OF PAINTINGS

AND PRINTS BY DAVID HOCKNEY

Whitworth Art Gallery, 1969
11¾ x 16½ in; 29.8 x 41.9 cm
Closing Scene, 1963

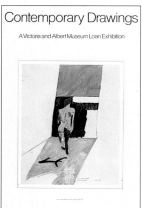

8 CONTEMPORARY DRAWINGS

A Victoria & Albert Museum Loan Exhibition, 1974
30½ x 20½ in; 77.5 x 52.1 cm
Man Running Towards a Bit of Blue, 1963

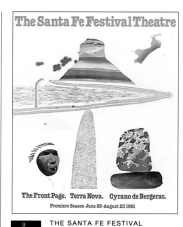

9 THE SANTA FE FESTIVAL

THEATRE

Santa Fe Festival Theatre, 1981
31¼ x 16½ in; 79.4 x 62.2 cm
Arizona, 1964

10 DAVID HOCKNEY:

SEVEN PAINTINGS

Tate Gallery London and Liverpool, 1992
30 x 20 in; 76.2 x 51
Man in Shower in Beverly Hills, 1964

11 A HOLLYWOOD COLLECTION

Editions Alecto, 1965
30¼ x 22 in; 76.6 x 56.2 cm
Hollywood Bowl, from *A Hollywood Collection*,
1965

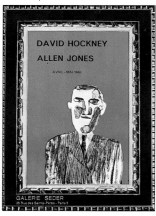

12 DAVID HOCKNEY ALLEN JONES

Galerie Seder, Paris, 1966
29 x 21½ in; 73.7 x 54.6 cm
Picture of a Portrait in a Silver Frame, from
A Hollywood Collection, 1965

13 POP ART: DAVID HOCKNEY

Royal Academy of Arts, 1991
23 x 31 in; 60 x 79 cm
Rocky Mountains and Tired Indians, 1965

14 UBU ROI

Royal Court Production, 1966
20 x 12½ in; 50.8 x 31.8 cm
Playbill for 'Ubu Roi', 1966

15 DAVID HOCKNEY COMPLETE

PRINTS

Galerie Mikro, Berlin, 1968
32 x 26½ in; 81.3 x 67.3 cm
Two Boys Aged 23 or 24, from *C.P. Cavafy*, 1966

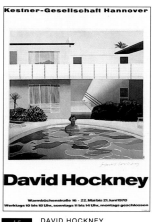

16 DAVID HOCKNEY

Kestner-Gesellschaft, Hannover, 1970
24 x 17 in; 61 x 43. cm
Portrait of Nick Wilder, 1966

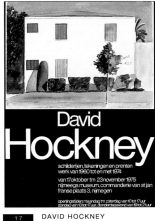

17 DAVID HOCKNEY

Nijmeegs Museum, 1974
27 x 19¼ in; 68.5 x 48.9 cm
House, Montana Blvd, 1967

18 DAVID HOCKNEY:

A BIGGER SPLASH

Tate Gallery, London, 1985
30 x 40½ in; 76.2 x 102.9 cm
Image also used: Metropolitan Museum of Art,
1988 (19)
A Bigger Splash, 1967

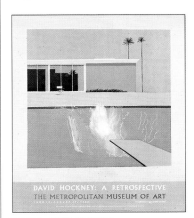

19 DAVID HOCKNEY:

A RETROSPECTIVE

Metropolitan Museum of Art, New York, 1988
33 x 28 in; 83.8 x 71.1 cm
Image also used: Tate Gallery, 1985 (18)
A Bigger Splash, 1967

20 1ST BRITISH INTERNATIONAL

PRINT BIENNALE

Bradford City Art Gallery, 1968
31½ x 24 in; 80 x 61 cm
Tree With Grass, 1968

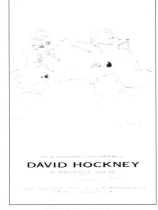

21 DAVID HOCKNEY:

A PRIVATE VIEW

Editions Graphiques Gallery, 1988
33 x 23 in; 85.6 x 59.4 cm
Peter, Aug, 68

22 LE TEMPS ET LA CHAMBRE

Odeon Theatre, 1991
23 x 15 in; 60 x 40 cm
Christopher Isherwood and Don Bachardy, 1968

23 DAVID HOCKNEY AT ANDRE EMMERICH

Andre Emmerich, New York, 1969
28 x 20 in; 71.1 x 50.8 cm
Reprinted by Petersburg Press, 1981
Corbusier Chair and Rug, 1969

24 DAVID HOCKNEY

Galerie Der Spiegel, Cologne, 1970
33 x 24 in; 83.8 x 61 cm
Reprinted by Petersburg Press, 1981
Image also used: by Galerie Eude, 1976 (27)
The Boy Hidden in an Egg, from *Grimm's Fairy
Tales*, 1969

25 DAVID HOCKNEY:

ILLUSTRATIONEN ZU GRIMM'S FAIRY TALES

Ziegler Editionen & Grafik, Zürich, 1971
30 x 20 in; 76.2 x 50.8 cm
He Tore Himself in Two, from *Grimm's Fairy Tales*, 1969

26 DAVID HOCKNEY: GRIMM'S

FAIRY TALES

A Victoria & Albert Loan Exhibition, 1974
30 x 20 in; 76.2 x 50.8 cm
Image also used: National Touring Exhibition, 1994 (32)
The Haunted Castle, from *Grimm's Fairy Tales*, 1969

27 DAVID HOCKNEY OBRA GRÀFICA 1961-74

Galerie Eude, Barcelona, 1976
26½ x 20½ in; 67.3 x 52.1 cm
Image also used: Galerie der Spiegel, 1970 (24)
The Boy Hidden in an Egg, from *Grimm's Fairy Tales*, 1969

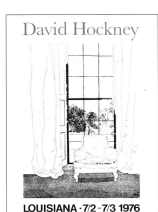

28 DAVID HOCKNEY

Louisiana, 1976
34 x 25 in; 86 x 63.2 cm
Image also used: Arun Art Centre, 1980 (30)
Home, from *Grimm's Fairy Tales*, 1969

29 DAVID HOCKNEY

Henie-Onstad Kunstsenter, Hovikodden, 1976
26½ x 19 in; 67.3 x 48.3 cm
Celia, 1969

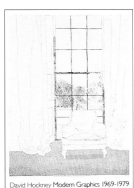

30 DAVID HOCKNEY: MODERN

GRAPHICS 1969-1979

Arun Art Centre, West Sussex, 1980
12 x 8 in; 32 x 20 cm
Image also used: Louisiana, 1976 (28)
Home, from *Grimm's Fairy Tales*, 1969

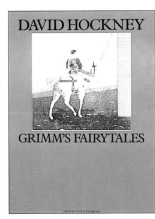

31 DAVID HOCKNEY: GRIMM'S

FAIRY TALES

British Council Touring Exhibition, 1984
22¾ x 16½ in; 57.8 x 41.9 cm
Rapunzel, Rapunzel, Let Down Your Hair, from
Grimm's Fairy Tales, 1969

32 DAVID HOCKNEY: GRIMM'S

FAIRY TALES

National Touring Exhibitions, 1994
16 x 11 in; 41.9 x 29.6 cm
Image also used: Victoria & Albert Loan Exhibiton,
1974 (26)
The Haunted Castle, from *Grimm's Fairy Tales*, 1969

33 DAVID HOCKNEY PAINTINGS,
PRINTS AND DRAWINGS 1960-1970

Whitechapel Art Gallery, 1970
26 x 19 in; 66 x 48.3 cm
Four Photos Based in Front of 'Le parc des sources', Vichy, 1970

34 OLYMPISCHE SPIELE MÜNCHEN 1972

Munich Olympic Games, 1972
39 x 25 in; 99.1 x 63.5 cm
Diver, 1970

35 DAVID HOCKNEY
ZEICHNUNGEN UND DRUCKGRAPHIK

Staatliche Graphische Sammlung, Munich, 1977
34 x 24 in; 86.4 x 61 cm
Peter with Scarf, 1970

36 DAVID HOCKNEY: TRAVELS WITH
PEN, PENCIL AND INK

The Fine Arts Museum, San Francisco, 1979
21¼ x 17 in; 53.3 x 42.2 cm
Sir John Geilgud, 1970

37 THE NINETEENTH NEW YORK
FILM FESTIVAL

New York Film Festival, 1981
39 x 27 in; 99.1 x 68.6 cm
Window, Grand Hotel, Vittel, 1970

38 VAN HENRY MOORE TOT
GILBERT & GEORGE

Europalia, Brussels, 1973
32¼ x 23 in; 82.6 x 58.4 cm
Mrs Clark, from Mr & Mrs Clark & Percy, 1970-71

39 NATIONAL COLLECTION OF
MODERN PAINTING

Tate Gallery, London, 1979
31½ x 21½ in; 80 x 54.6 cm
Mr Clark, from Mr & Mrs Clark & Percy, 1970-71

40 HOCKNEY PRINTS

Caius Art Gallery, Cambridge, 1976
33 x 21 in; 83.8 x 53.3 cm
Paris, 27 rue de Seine, 1971

41 OPERA GRAFICHE DI DAVID
HOCKNEY

Galleria del Cavallino, Venice, 1981
28 x 20½ in; 71.1 x 52.1 cm
Detail from Mark, Bella Vista Hotel, Macao, 1971

42 LOUISIANA MUSEUM FOR MODERNE
KUNST/MUSEUM OF CONTEMPORARY ART

Humlebaek, Denmark, 1987
34 x 25 in; 86.3 x 63.3 cm
Pool and Steps, Le Nid de Duc, 1971

43 DAVID HOCKNEY: A RETROSPECTIVE

Metropolitan Museum of Art, New York, 1988
30 x 37 in; 76.4 x 93.9 cm
Portrait of the Artist (Pool with Two Figures), 1971

44 DAVID HOCKNEY: A RETROSPECTIVE

Los Angeles County Museum of Art, 1988
38 x 23 in; 97.5 x 60.5 cm
Beach Umbrella, 1971

45 THE THREEPENNY OPERA

Prince of Wales Theatre, London, 1972
24 x 13 in; 62.2 x 33 cm
Playbill for 'The Threepenny Opera', 1972

46 THE METROPOLITAN MUSEUM
OF ART DEPARTMENT OF TWENTIETH
CENTURY ART

Metropolitan Museum of Art, New York, 1972
37 x 25 in; 94 x 63.5 cm
Image also used: Fundación Juan March, 1992 (52)
Mount Fuji, 1972

47 TRAVELS WITH PEN, PENCIL
AND INK: PRINTS AND DRAWINGS BY
DAVID HOCKNEY

Portland Centre for Visual Arts, 1978
12 x 23 in; 32.4 x 59.1 cm
The Artist's Mother, 1972

48 DAVID HOCKNEY: TRAVELS WITH
PEN, PENCIL AND INK

Tate Gallery, London, 1980
30 x 20 in; 76.2 x 50.8 cm
Celia in a Black Dress with White Flowers, 1972

49   DAVID HOCKNEY PHOTOGRAPHE

Pompidou Centre, Paris, 1982
27½ x 20 in; 69.9 x 50.8 cm
Image also used: Frankfurter Kunstverein, 1983 (50)
Peter, Kensington Gardens, April 1972

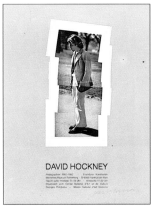

50   DAVID HOCKNEY PHOTOGRAPHIEN

1962-1982
Frankfurter Kunstverein, 1983
33 x 23½ in; 83.8 x 59.7 cm
Image also used: Pompidou Centre,1982 (49)
Peter, Kensington Gardens, April 1972

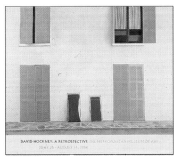

51   DAVID HOCKNEY;

A RETROSPECTIVE
Metropolitan Museum of Art, New York, 1988
30 x 32 in; 76.4 x 83.3 cm
Image also used: Palau de la Virreina, 1993 (53)
Two Deck Chairs, Calvi, 1972

52   DAVID HOCKNEY

Fundación Juan March, Madrid, 1992
37 x 22 in; 95 x 56 cm
Image also used: Metropolitan Museum of Art,
1972 (46)
Mount Fuji, 1972

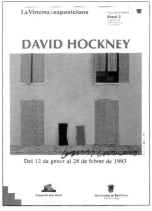

53   DAVID HOCKNEY

Palau de la Virreina, Barcelona, 1993
19 x 13 in; 49.9 x 35 cm
Also used: Metropolitan Museum of Art,
New York, 1988 (51)
Two Deck Chairs, Calvi, 1972

54   DAVID HOCKNEY

Europalia, Brussels, 1973
28½ x 22in; 72.4 x 55.9 cm
Mirror, Casa Santini, Lucca, 1973

55   AN ETCHING AND A

LITHOGRAPH FOR EDITIONS ALECTO
Editions Alecto, 1973
38 x 27½ in; 96.5 x 69.9 cm
*An Etching and a Lithograph for Editions
Alecto*, 1973

56   DAVID HOCKNEY AT ANDRE

EMMERICH
Andre Emmerich, New York, 1973
29 x 24 in; 75.6 x 61 cm
Still Life with Book, 1973

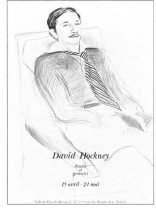

57   DAVID HOCKNEY DESSINS ET

GRAVURES
Galerie Claude Bernard, Paris, 1975
25¼ x 17¾ in; 64.1 x 45.1 cm
Jacques de Bascher de Beaumarchais, 1973

58   DAVID HOCKNEY PRINTS 1954-77

Scottish Arts Council Touring Exhibition, 1977
30 x 20½ in; 76.2 x 52.1 cm
Reprinted by Petersburg Press, 1981 (60)
Sun, from *Weather Series*, 1973

59   CONTEMPORARY BRITISH

DRAWINGS
Tel Aviv Museum, Tel Aviv, 1980
28 x 20½ in; 71.1 x 52.1 cm
Celia in a Black Dress and Lace Collar, 1973

60   DAVID HOCKNEY PRINTS 1954-77

Reprint by Petersburg Press, 1981, of Scottish
Arts Council Touring Exhibition, 1977 (58)
37¾ x 27 in; 95.9 x 68.6 cm
Sun, from *Weather Series*, 1973

61   DAVID HOCKNEY DRAWINGS

Rex Irwin Art Dealer, Sydney, 1981
36 x 26 in; 91.5 x 66 cm
Image also used: Petersburg Press; Thorden
Wetterling, Gothenburg
Celia Wearing Checked Sleeves, 1973

62   DAVID HOCKNEY ZEICHNUNGEN

UND GRAFIK
Galerie Kammer, Hamburg, 1981
35 x 25 in; 88.9 x 63.5 cm
Celia in a Black Dress with a Coloured Border, 1973

63   DAVID HOCKNEY, PRINT

RETROSPECTIVE
Thorden Wetterling, Gothenburg, 1984
39½ x 27½ in; 100.3 x 69.9 cm
Image also used: Canberra, 1976
Celia, 8365 Melrose Avenue, 1973

64   DAVID HOCKNEY, PRINT

RETROSPECTIVE
Thorden Wetterling, Stockholm, 1984
39 x 27 in; 100 x 70 cm
Celia, 1973

65 A BIGGER SPLASH

Poster for 'A Bigger Splash' film, 1974
31 x 41 in; 78.7 x 104.1 cm
Peter Schlesinger and Figure Swimming, from
Pool with Two Figures, 1974

66 DAVID HOCKNEY

Musée des Arts Décoratifs, Paris, 1974
25½ x 19½ in; 64.8 x 49.5 cm
Two Vases in the Louvre, 1974

67 DAVID HOCKNEY: AN EXHIBITION
OF COSTUME DRAWINGS AND SET DESIGNS

Ashmolean Museum, Oxford, 1981
30 x 38 in; 76.2 x 96.5 cm
Image also used: Japanese Touring Exhibition,
1992-3 (68)
Curtain for *'The Rake's Progress'*, Epilogue, 1974-5

68 HOCKNEY'S OPERA

Japanese Touring Exhibition 1992-3
Image also used: Ashmolean Museum, 1981 (67)
28 x 20 in; 72.6 x 51.4 cm
Curtain for *'The Rake's Progress'*, Epilogue, 1974-5

69 GLYNDEBOURNE TOURING OPERA

Bristol City Art Gallery, Manchester City Art
Gallery, 1975
25 x 16½ in; 63.5 x 41.9 cm
Glyndebourne Touring Opera, 1975

70 KUNST DER GEGENWART

Staatliche Graphische Sammlung, Munich, 1977
33 x 23½ in; 83.8 x 59.7 cm
Clive Barker, 1975

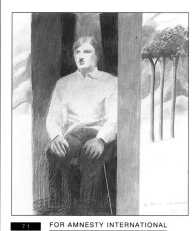

71 FOR AMNESTY INTERNATIONAL

Amnesty International, 1977
28½ x 23¼ in; 72.4 x 59.1 cm
Prisoner, 1975

72 ZEICHNUNGEN UND
DRUCKGRAPHIK 1960-1977

Salzburg Künstlerhaus, Salzburg, 1978
35 x 25 in; 88.9 x 63.5 cm
Image also used: Albertina Vienna; Tiroler
Landesmuseum, Innsbruck: Kulturhaus der
Stadt, Graz
Gregory and Mark, 1975

73 SAN FRANCISCO OPERA

SUMMER FESTIVAL SEASON, 1982

San Francisco Opera, 1982
39 x 34 in; 99.1 x 86.4 cm
Image also used: Hockney's Opera Japanese
Exhibition, 1992 (74)
Detail of *Bedlam*, from *'The Rake's Progress'*, 1975

74 HOCKNEY'S OPERA JAPANESE

TOURING EXHIBITION 1992-3

Image also used: San Francisco Opera
Summer Festival Season, 1982 (73)
28 x 20 in; 72.6 x 51.4 cm
Detail of *Bedlam*, from *'The Rake's Progress'*, 1975

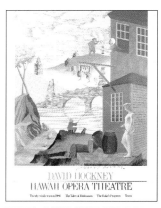

75 HAWAII OPERA THEATRE 1986

26 x 20 in; 66.1 x 50.8 cm
Kerby (After Hogarth) Useful Knowledge, 1975

76 SPOLETO FESTIVAL

Spoleto, 1976
40 x 28 in; 102.9 x 72.4 cm
Simplified Faces, 1976

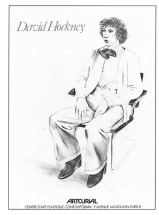

77 DAVID HOCKNEY

Artcurial, Paris, 1979
30 x 21 in; 76.2 x 53.3 cm
Gregory Evans, 1976

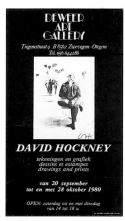

78 DAVID HOCKNEY

Deweer Art Gallery, 1986
19½ x 10¾ in; 49.5 x 27.3 cm
Henry Seated with Tulips, 1976

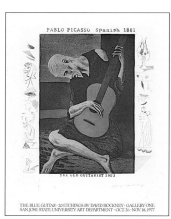

79 THE BLUE GUITAR: 20 ETCHINGS

BY DAVID HOCKNEY

San Jose State University Art Department, 1977
23½ x 18½ in; 59.7 x 47 cm
The Old Guitarist, from *'The Blue Guitar'*, 1976-7

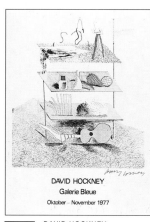

80 DAVID HOCKNEY

Galerie Bleue, 1977
31¼ x 23 in; 79.4 x 58.4 cm
Image also used: Victoria & Albert Museum, 1985 (83)
Serenade, from *'The Blue Guitar'*, 1976-7

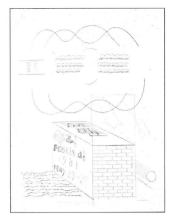

81 OJAI FESTIVAL 1981

30 x 22 in; 76 x 56 cm

The Buzzing of the Blue Guitar, from *'The Blue Guitar'*, 1976-7

82 HOCKNEY: THE BLUE GUITAR

Meta Galleria, Florence, 1981

28½ x 21 in; 72.4 x 53.3 cm

The Poet, from *'The Blue Guitar'*, 1976-7

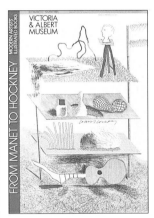

83 FROM MANET TO HOCKNEY: MODERN ARTISTS' ILLUSTRATED BOOKS

Victoria & Albert Museum, London, 1985

30 x 20 in; 76.2 x 50.8 cm

Image also used: Galerie Bleue, 1977 (80)

Serenade, from *'The Blue Guitar'*, 1976-7

84 DAVID HOCKNEY AT ANDRE EMMERICH

Andre Emmerich, New York, 1977

26½ x 24 in; 67.3 x 61 cm

Self Portrait with Blue Guitar, 1977

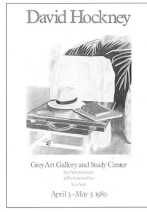

85 DAVID HOCKNEY

Grey Art Gallery, New York, 1980

28 x 19¾ in; 71.1 x 50.2 cm

Reprinted by Petersburg Press, 1981 (86)

Taj Hotel, Bombay, 1977

86 DAVID HOCKNEY

Grey Art Gallery, New York, 1980

37½ x 27 in; 95.3 x 69.2 cm

Reprint by Petersburg Press (85)

Taj Hotel, Bombay, 1977

87 THE ARTIST'S EYE

National Gallery, London, 1981

30 x 20 in; 76.2 x 50.8 cm

Looking at Pictures on a Screen, 1977

88 THE BLUE GUITAR: ETCHINGS BY DAVID HOCKNEY

British Council Touring Exhibition, 1983

23¼ x 16½ in; 59 x 41.9 cm

The Blue Guitar, from *'The Blue Guitar'* 1977

89 DASH

His Majesty's Theatre, Aberdeen, 1985

23¼ x 16½ in; 59 x 41.9 cm

Two Dancers, 1977

90 DAVID HOCKNEY PISCINES DE PAPIER: PAPER POOLS

Editions Herscher, 1980

26 x 20 in; 66 x 50.8 cm

Image also used: Editions Herscher, 1980 (91); Metropolitan Museum of Art, 1988 (94)

Day Pool with Three Blues, 1978 (Paper Pool No 7)

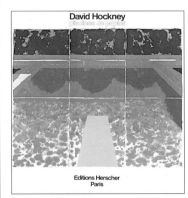

91 DAVID HOCKNEY PISCINES DE PAPIER: PAPER POOLS

Editions Herscher, 1980

Published by Petersburg Press

37¾ x 34½ in; 95.9 x 87.6 cm

Image also used: Editions Herscher, 1980 (90); Metropolitan Museum of Art, 1988 (94)

Day Pool with Three Blues, 1978 (Paper Pool No 7)

92 HOCKNEY'S PROGRESS

Graves Art Gallery, Sheffield, 1980

28 x 22½ in; 71.1 x 57.2 cm

The Artist's Mother, 1978

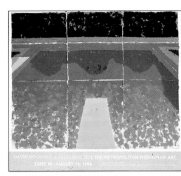

93 THE AUSTRALIAN NATIONAL GALLERY, CANBERRA

Australian National Gallery, Canberra, 1982

32 x 52½ in; 81.3 x 133.4 cm

A Diver, from *Paper Pools*, 1978

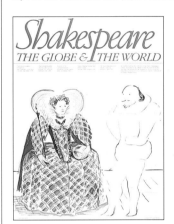

94 DAVID HOCKNEY: A RETROSPECTIVE

Metropolitan Museum of Art, New York, 1988

30 x 31 in; 76.3 x 78.8 cm

Image also used: Editions Herscher, 1980 (90, 91)

Day Pool with Three Blues, 1978 (Paper Pool No 7)

95 SHAKESPEARE: THE GLOBE AND THE WORLD

USA Exhibition, 1979

30½ x 21½ in; 77.5 x 54.6 cm

Elizabeth and Shakespeare, 1979

96 THE LADY AND THE CLARINET

Mark Taper Forum, 1980

22 x 14 in; 55.8 x 35.5 cm

Celia Musing, 1979

97 LOS ANGELES BICENTENNIAL

1781 1981

Los Angeles, 1981
32 x 26½ in; 81.3 x 67.3 cm
Skaters, Venice, 1979

98 DAVID'S EVENING ON WHEELS

New York, 1980
29½ x 21½ in; 74.9 x 54.6 cm
Roller Skates, 1980

99 PARIS REVIEW 25TH

ANNIVERSARY 1981

35 x 26 in; 88.9 x 66 cm
Flower Study, 1980

100 DAVID HOCKNEY

Galerie Claude Bernard, Paris, 1981
24½ x 17 in; 62.2 x 43.2 cm
Image also used: Walker Art Center, 1983
(112); Museo Tamayo, 1984 (116); Toronto,
1984
Les Mamelles de Tirésias, 1980

101 PAINTINGS AND DRAWINGS FOR

THE METROPOLITAN OPERA'S 'PARADE'

Andre Emmerich, New York, 1981
39 x 27 in; 99.1 x 68.6 cm
Image also used: Riverside Studios Exhibition, 1981
Set for 'Parade', 1980

102 THE PARADE POSTER

Metropolitan Opera, New York, 1981
38 x 23¾ in; 96.5 x 60.3 cm
Harlequin, 1980

103 PARADE

Metropolitan Opera, New York, 1981
84 x 49 in; 213.4 x 124.5 cm
Image also used: Pavilion Books,1987;
Harmony Books, 1987; Japanese Touring
Exhibition, 1987 (119)
Harlequin, 1980

104 IGOR STRAVINSKY:

METROPOLITAN OPERA

New York, 1981
38 x 17 in; 96.5 x 43.2 cm
Also larger version 84 x 49 in; 124.5 x 213.4 cm
Stravinsky, 1980

105 CITY OF LONDON BARBICAN

CENTRE FOR THE ARTS

Barbican Centre, London, 1982
37½ x 28½ in; 95.3 x 72.4 cm
Detail from *Cubistic Bar*, 1980

106 THE NEW WORLD FESTIVAL OF

THE ARTS

Miami, 1982
38½ x 35¾ in; 97.8 x 90.8 cm
Detail from *The Zanzibar with Postcards*
Kiosk Bodega version, 1980

107 YOUNG PLAYWRIGHTS' FESTIVAL

New York, 1982
41 x 30¼ in; 104.1 x 76.8 cm
Image also used: Thames and Hudson, 1983
(113)
Detail from *Pulcinella with Applause*, 1980

108 DAVID HOCKNEY DRAWINGS

FOR THE THEATRE

Nishimura Gallery, Tokyo, 1982
36½ x 32 in; 92.7 x 81.3 cm
Detail from *'Parade'*, 1980

109 A FRENCH TRIPLE BILL POSTER

Metropolitan Opera House, New York, 1982
80 x 41 in; 203.2 x 104 cm
Triple Bill: *The Right of Spring, Le Rossignol*
and *Oedipus Rex*, 1980

110 HOCKNEY PAINTS THE STAGE

Walker Art Center, 1983
27 x 37 in; 68.6 x 94 cm
Image also used: Fort Worth, San Francisco
Two Dancers, 1980

111 THE NIGHTINGALE

AND L'ENFANT ET LES SORTILÈGES

Royal Opera House, Covent Garden, London,
1983
30 x 20 in; 76.2 x 50.8 cm
The Nightingale, 1981, and *L'enfant et les
sortilèges*, 1980

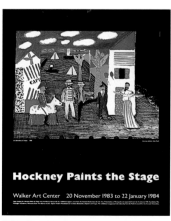

112 HOCKNEY PAINTS THE STAGE

Walker Art Center, 1983
34 x 24 in; 86.4 x 61 cm
Image also used: Galerie Claude Bernard, 1981
(100); Museo Tamayo, 1984 (116); Toronto,
1984
Les Mamelles de Tirésias, 1980

113   HOCKNEY PAINTS THE STAGE

Thames and Hudson, 1983
23½ x 16½ in; 59.7 x 41.9 cm
Image also used: Young Playwrights' Festival,
New York, 1982 (107)
Detail from *Pulcinella with Applause*, 1980

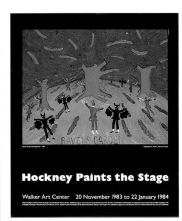

114   HOCKNEY PAINTS THE STAGE

Walker Art Center, 1983
34½ x 27½ in; 87.6 x 69.9 cm
Image also used: Museo Tamayo, 1984 (117)
Ravel's Garden with Night Glow, 1980

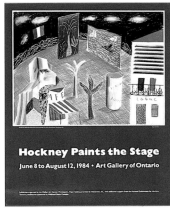

115   HOCKNEY PAINTS THE STAGE

Art Gallery of Ontario, 1984
24 x 30 in; 61 x 76 cm
Detail from *The Zanzibar with Postcards and
Kiosk Tabac version*, 1980

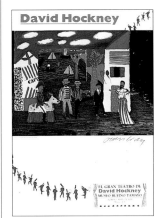

116   DAVID HOCKNEY

Museo Tamayo, Mexico City, 1984
35¼ x 23½ in; 89.5 x 59.7 cm
Image also used: Galerie Claude Bernard, 1981 (100);
Walker Art Center, 1983 (112); Toronto, 1984
Les Mamelles de Tirésias, 1980

117   DAVID HOCKNEY

Museo Tamayo, Mexico City, 1984
35½ x 23 in; 89.5 x 58.4 cm
Image also used: Walker Art Center, 1983 (114)
Ravel's Garden with Night Glow, 1980

118   HOCKNEY PAINTS THE STAGE

Hayward Gallery, 1985
40 x 56¼ in; 101.6 x 143 cm
Detail from *The Garden with Singers*, 1980

119   HOCKNEY POSTERS

Japanese Touring Exhibition, 1987
40 – 28 in; 103 x 73 cm
Image also used: Metropolitan Opera, 1981
(103); Pavilion Books,1987; Harmony Books,
1987
Harlequin, 1980

120   MULHOLLAND DRIVE: THE ROAD
TO THE STUDIO

Los Angeles County Museum of Art, 1987
16 x 38 in; 42.6 x 96.5 cm
Mulholland Drive: The Road to the Studio, 1980

121   DAVID HOCKNEY:
A RETROSPECTIVE

Metropolitan Museum of Art, New York, 1988
25 x 42 in; 63.8 x 106.6 cm
Hollywood Hills House, 1980

122   DAVID HOCKNEY:
A RETROSPECTIVE

Metropolitan Museum of Art, New York, 1988
39 x 24 in; 99 x 61 cm
Nichol's Canyon, 1980

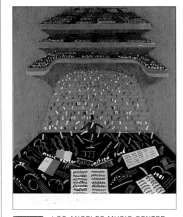

123   LOS ANGELES MUSIC CENTER
UNIFIED FUND, 1981

28 x 22½ in; 71.1 x 57.2 cm
Interior of Music Center Los Angeles, 1981

124   AUSTRALIAN NATIONAL GALLERY

32 – 22 in; 82.3 x 56 cm
Potted Daffodils, 1981

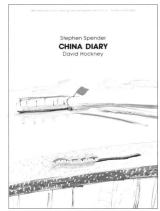

125   CHINA DIARY

Thames and Hudson, 1982
23½ x 16½ in; 59.7 x 41.9 cm
Kweilin, 1981

126   DAVID HOCKNEY

Museo Tamayo, Mexico City, 1984
35 x 23½ in; 88.9 x 59.7 cm
Courtiers and Masks, 1981

127   DAVID HOCKNEY, SEIBU,
TOKYO, 1988

14 x 20; 36.5 x 51.5 cm
Kweilin Airport, 1981

128   DAVID HOCKNEY

Seibu, Tokyo, 1988
Image also used: Parco, 1988
40 x 28 in; 103 x 72.7 cm
Tiananmen Square and Imperial Palace, 1981

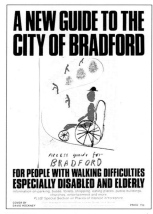

129 A NEW GUIDE TO THE
CITY OF BRADFORD

Bradford, 1982
25 x 17 in; 63.5 x 43.2 cm
Access Guide for Bradford, 1982

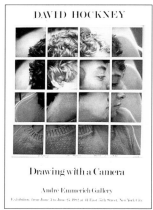

130 DAVID HOCKNEY; DRAWING
WITH A CAMERA

Andre Emmerich Gallery, New York, 1982
39 x 27 in ; 99.1 x 68.6 cm
Gregory, Los Angeles, March 1982

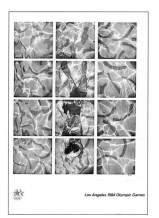

131 LOS ANGELES 1984 OLYMPIC
GAMES

36 x 24 in; 91.4 x 61 cm
Polaroids of Swimmer, 1982

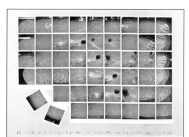

132 IN COLOR: TEN CALIFORNIAN
PHOTOGRAPHERS

The Oakland Museum, 1983
34 x 42½ in; 86 x 115 cm
Ian Swimming; Los Angeles, 11 March 1982

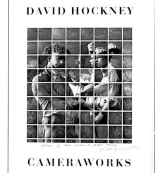

133 DAVID HOCKNEY: CAMERAWORKS

Thames and Hudson, 1984
23½ x 16½ in ; 59.7 x 41.9 cm
Detail from *Paul Kasmin & Jasper Conran,
Pembroke Studios London, 8 May, 1982*

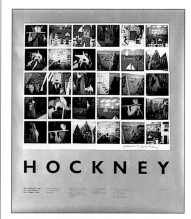

134 HOCKNEY PAINTS THE STAGE

Art Gallery of Ontario, 1984
36 x 30 in; 91.4 x 76.2 cm
*Painting and Sculpting the Stage, Composite
Polaroid, 1982*

135 XIV WINTER OLYMPIC GAMES

Sarajevo, Yugoslavia, 1984
26 x 19½ in ; 66 x 49.5 cm
Skater, New York, 1982

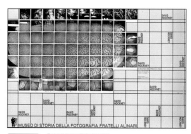

136 DAVID HOCKNEY

Museo de Storia Fotografia Fratelli Alinari,
Florence, 1985
27 x 39½ in; 68.6 x 100.3 cm
Rain on the Pool, Los Angeles, 1982

137 HOCKNEY'S PHOTOGRAPHS

British Touring Exhibition, Japan, 1986
28½ x 20¼ in; 72.4 x 51.4 cm
*Photographing Annie Liebovitz While She
Photographs Me, February 1983* and *Gregory
Swimming, Los Angeles, March 1982*

138 DAVID HOCKNEY

British Council Touring Exhibition, Japan, 1986
28½ x 20¼ in ; 72.4 x 51.4 cm
Telegraph Pole, Los Angeles, September 1982

139 HOCKNEY'S PHOTOGRAPHS

British Council Touring Exhibition, Japan, 1986
20¼ x 14¼ in; 51.4 x 36.2 cm
*My Mother Sleeping, Los Angeles, December
1982*

140 DAVID HOCKNEY: PHOTOCOLLAGES

Santa Monica College Photography Gallery, 1988
24 x 36 in; 61 x 91.4 cm
The Steering Wheel, October 1982

141 VENICE FAMILY CLINIC ART
WALK '83

Art Walk, 1983
25½ x 34½ in; 64.8 x 87.6 cm
Gregory Walking, 1983

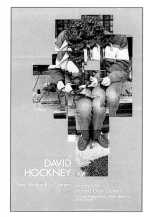

142 DAVID HOCKNEY; NEW WORK
WITH A CAMERA

Richard Gray Gallery, Chicago, 1983
39 x 25 in; 99.1 x 63.5 cm
Gregory Loading His Camera, 1983

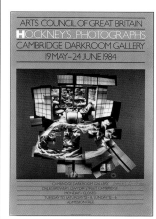

143 HOCKNEY'S PHOTOGRAPHS

Cambridge Darkroom Gallery, 1983
30 x 20 in; 76.2 x 50.8 cm
Image also used: touring exhibition in
Bradford, Milton Keynes, Bath and London
Gregory Watching the Snow Fall, Kyoto, 1983

144 THE NATIONAL TRUST
FOUNTAINS ABBEY APPEAL

National Trust, 1984
30 x 20 in; 76.2 x 50.8 cm
Ian; Fountains Abbey, January 1983

145 ARTISTS DESIGN FOR DANCE

1909-84

Arnolfini, Bristol, 1984
23½ x 33 in; 60 x 84 cm
Vari Capricci, 1983

146 DAVID HOCKNEY FOTOGRAFO

Fundacao Calouste Gulbenkian, Lisbon, 1985
26½ x 18½ in; 67.3 x 47 cm
Detail of *Don Bachardy*, from *Christopher Isherwood Talking to Bob Holman, Santa Monica*, March 1983

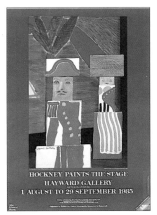

147 HOCKNEY PAINTS THE STAGE

Hayward Gallery, 1985
30 x 20 in; 76.2 x 50.8 cm
Detail from *Les Mamelles de Tirésias*, 1983

148 DAVID HOCKNEY: L'ENFANT ET LES SORTILEGES

The Contemporary Museum, Honolulu, Hawaii, 1989
26 x 20 in; 66 x 51.9 cm
The little Princess coming out of the book of fairytales, 1983

149 THE MAGIC FLUTE

Michigan Opera Theatre, 1991
26 x 18 in; 66 x 46 cm
Detail from the theatre set of 'The Magic Flute' exhibition in the *Hockney Paints the Stage* travelling exhbition, 1983

150 XVI RIP ARLES

Arles, 1985
42½ x 28½ in; 108 x 72.4 cm
Nude, 16 June 1984

151 CONTENT + CONTEXT: PHOTOGRAPHY AND THE FINE ARTS, 1985

19½ x 39¾ in; 49.5 x 101 cm
Walking Past Le Rossignol, April, 1984

152 HOCKNEY FOTOGRAFO, 1985

Sala de Exposiciones de la Caja de Pensiones, 1985
24½ x 16¾ in; 62.2 x 42.5 cm
Also used: British Council Touring Exhibition, Japan, 1986 (154); British Council Touring Exhibition, 1987 (155)
The Desk, London, 1 July 1984

153 NINTH BRITISH INTERNATIONAL PRINT BIENNALE

Cartwright Hall, 1986
30 x 20 in; 76.2 x 50. 8 cm
Pembroke Studio with Blue Chairs and Lamp, 1984

154 HOCKNEY

British Council Touring Exhibition, Japan, 1986
28¾ x 20¼ in; 73 x 52.7 cm
Image also used: Sala de Exposiciones de la Caja de Pensiones, 1985 (152); British Council Touring Exhibition Australasia, 1987 (155)
The Desk, London, 1 July 1984

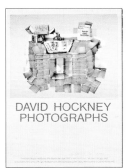

155 DAVID HOCKNEY PHOTOGRAPHS

British Council Touring Exhibition, Australasia, 1987
34 x 23 in; 87 x 60 cm
Also used: Sala de Exposiciones de la Caja de Pensiones, 1985 (152); British Council Touring Exhibition, Japan, 1986 (154)
The Desk, London, 1 July, 1984

156 DAVID HOCKNEY: A RETROSPECTIVE

Metropolitan Museum of Art, New York, 1988
25 x 28 in; 64.6 x 70.9 cm
Three Pictures, Study for Chair IV (1984)

157 DAVID HOCKNEY MOVING FOCUS PRINTS

Tyler Graphics, Tate Gallery, 1986
32 x 22 in; 81.3 x 55.9 cm
Image also used: Artium, 1989 (158, 159); Tate Gallery, 1994 (160)
View of Hotel Well III, 1985

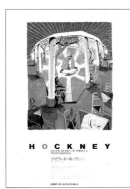

158 HOCKNEY MAJOR WORKS OF PRINTS AND PHOTOGRAPHS

Art Gallery Artium, 1989
40 x 28 in; 102.6 x 72.5 cm
Image also used: Tate Gallery, 1986 (157); Artium, 1989 (159); Tate Gallery, 1994 (160)
Views of Hotel Well III, 1985

159 DAVID HOCKNEY: GRAPHICS AND PHOTOCOLLAGES, 1965-88

Art Gallery Artium, 1989
33 x 23 in; 83.9 x 59 cm
Image also used: Tate Gallery, 1986 (157); Artium, 1989 (158); Tate Gallery, 1994 (160)
View of Hotel Well III, 1985

160 CONTEMPORARY PRINTS

Tate Gallery, London, 1994
30 x 20 in; 763 x 510 cm
Image also used: Tate Gallery, 1986 (157); Artium, 1989 (158, 159)
View of Hotel Well III, 1985

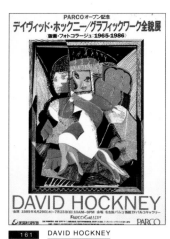

161 DAVID HOCKNEY

Parco Gallery, Japan, 1989
40 x 28 in; 102.6 x 72.5 cm
An Image of Celia, 1984-86

162 VOGUE PARIS PAR DAVID
HOCKNEY

Cover: newsstand version, 1985
15½ x 11¾ in; 39.5 x 30 cm
Tableau de David Hockney, 1985

163 DAVID HOCKNEY; IMAGES ET
PENSÉES POUR LE MAGAZINE VOGUE PARIS

Galerie Claude Bernard, Paris, 1985
32 x 19 in; 50.2 x 82.6 cm
Detail of Gregory, 1985

164 ON A BESOIN DE PLUS
GRANDES PERSPECTIVES

Arles, 1985
22 x 29 57.2 x 74.9 cm
On a besoin de plus grandes perspectives
(Wider perspectives are needed now), 1985

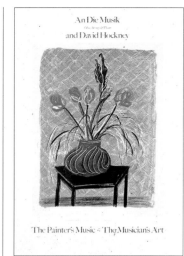

165 AN DIE MUSIK AND DAVID
HOCKNEY, 1985

39 x 26 in; 98.9 x 67.1 cm
Image also used: Thorden Wetterling Galleries,
1986 (166); Christies Contemporary Art, 1990
(173)
Amaryllis in Vase, 1985

166 PRINTS FROM TYLER GRAPHICS,
1984-6

Thorden Wetterling Galleries, Gothenburg,
1986
39 x 24 in; 99.8 x 63 cm
Image also used: An Die Musik and David
Hockney 1985 (165); Christies Contemporary
Art,1990 (173)
Amaryllis in Vase, 1985

167 DAVID HOCKNEY:
A RETROSPECTIVE

Los Angles County Museum of Art, 1988
18 x 39 in; 45.6 x 100.* cm
Image also used: Thames & Hudson, 1988
A Walk Around the Hotel Courtyard, Acatalan, 1985

168 DAVID HOCKNEY: A RETROSPECTIVE

Metropolitan Museum of Art, New York, 1988
28 x 35 in; 71 x 88.9 cm
Image also used: Jonathan Cape, 1988 (172)
Terrace without Shadows, 1985

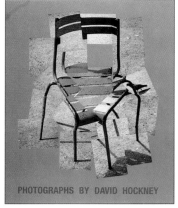

169 PHOTOGRAPHS BY DAVID
HOCKNEY

Touring exhibition by the International
Exhibitions Foundation, Washington DC, 1988
28 x 22 in; 71.1 x 55.9 cm
Chair, Jardin de Luxembourg, 7 August 1985

170 HOCKNEY AT ART CENTER, 1988

15 x 40 in; 39.1 x 101.6
Hotel Acatalan, Second Day, 1985

171 DAVID HOCKNEY AT THE JUNIOR
ARTS CENTER, COTSEN FELLOW,1988

Barnsdall Art Park, Los Angeles
39 x 25 in; 99 x 63.5 cm
The Chair, 1985

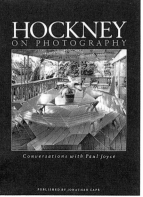

172 HOCKNEY ON PHOTOGRAPHY:
CONVERSATIONS WITH PAUL JOYCE

Jonathan Cape, 1988
23 x 16 in; 59.3 x 42 cm
Image also used: Metropolitan Museum of Art,
1988 (168)
Terrace without Shadows, 1985

173 DAVID HOCKNEY: 25 YEARS OF
PRINTMAKING

Christies Contemporary Art 1990
23 x 16 in; 59.1 x 42.1 cm
Image also used: An Die Musik and David
Hockney, 1985 (165); Thorden Wetterling
Galleries, 1985 (166)
Amaryllis in Vase, 1985

174 DAVID HOCKNEY: GRAPHICS
AND PHOTOCOLLAGES 1965-88

Art Gallery Artium, 1989
14 x 20 in; 36.4 x 51.5 cm
Hotel Acatalan: Two Weeks Later, 1985-6

175 DAVID HOCKNEY
PHOTOCOLLAGES

The Tel Aviv Museum, Helena Rubenstein
Pavillion, 1986-7
34 x 42 in; 86.5 x 115 cm
Paint Trolley, 1986

176 DAVID HOCKNEY
PHOTOCOLLAGES

International Center of Photography, New York,
1986
32 x 36 in; 82 x 92.7 cm
Pearblossom Highway, 11-18 April 1986

177 TENTH ANNIVERSARY SAN
FRANCISCO GIRLS' CHORUS, 1988

39 x 17 in; 101 x 43.1 cm
The Red Pot, April, 1986, from *Home Made Prints*

178 FIESTA '88

12th June 1988, St James' Market, Bradford
24 x 16 in; 63 x 42.9 cm
Flowers, Apple & Pear on a Table, July 1986, from *Home Made Prints*

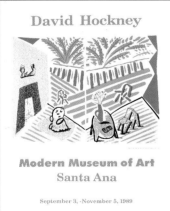

179 DAVID HOCKNEY

Modern Museum of Art, Santa Ana, 1989
36 x 26 in; 91.4 x 66.1 cm
Living Room & Terrace, 1986, from *Home Made Prints*

180 ART FOR EQUALITY

ICA Nash Rooms, 1991
23 x 16 in; 59.5 x 42.4 cm
Red Flowers and Blue Spots, 1986

181 HOCKNEY'S OPERA

Japanese Touring Exhibition, 1992-3
28 x 20 in; 72.6 x 51.5 cm
'Tristan and Isolde' Model of the Ship for Act I, 1986-7

182 LOS ANGELES MUSIC CENTER
OPERA, 1987

39 x 20 in; 98.9 x 51 cm
Tristan und Isolde I, 1987

183 DAVID HOCKNEY:
A RETROSPECTIVE

Tate Gallery, London, 1988
28 x 20 in; 70.9 x 50.6 cm
Little Stanley Sleeping, 1987

184 DAVID HOCKNEY:
A RETROSPECTIVE

Los Angeles County Museum of Art, 1988
40 x 21 in; 101.5 x 53 cm
Still Life With Magenta Curtain, 1987

185 HOCKNEY: HOME MADE PRINTS

The Cleveland Center for Contemporary Art, 1989
23 x 11 in; 58.5 x 28 cm
Self Portrait, July 1987, from *Home Made Prints*

186 DAVID HOCKNEY:
A RETROSPECTIVE

Metropolitan Museum of Art, New York, 1988
31 x 26 in; 78.5 x 66 cm
Still Life with Flowers, 1988

187 DAVID HOCKNEY:
A RETROSPECTIVE

Tate Gallery, London, 1988
30 x 20 in; 76.7 x 50.7 cm
My Mother, Bridlington, 1988

188 ART AGAINST AIDS

Los Angeles, 1988
24 x 18 in; 61 x 46 cm
Bowl of Fruit and Spotted Floor, 1988

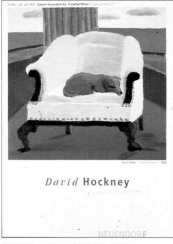

189 DAVID HOCKNEY: RECENT
PAINTINGS

Galerie Neuendorf, Frankfurt, 1989
33 x 21 in; 84 x 54.9 cm
Chair with Stanley, August, 1988

190 DAVID HOCKNEY

1853 Gallery, Salts Mill, Bradford, 1989
27 x 32in; 70 x 83.4 cm
Montcalm Interior at Seven O'Clock, 1988

191 INTERNATIONAL GARDEN AND
GREENERY EXPOSITION

Tsurumi Ryokuchi, Osaka, 1990
28 x 20 in; 72.6 x 51.2 cm
One Lavender Petunia, 1988

192 DAVID HOCKNEY: FAX, 1990

Centro Cultural Arte Contemporaneo AC Mexico
36 x 25 in; 92.9 x 63.3 cm
Untitled Image, 1988

193 DAVID HOCKNEY: FAX, 1990

Centro Cultural Arte Contemporaneo AC
Mexico
36 x 25 in; 92.9 x 63.3 cm
Untitled Image, 1988

194 20TH CENTURY ART, DAVID
HOCKNEY

Metropolitan Museum of Art, 1991
28 x 42 in; 71.5 x 106.6 cm
Large Interior, Los Angeles, 1988

195 DAVID HOCKNEY

Palais des Beaux-Arts, Brussels/
Paleis Voor Schone Kunsten, 1992
French and Flemmish captioned posters
23 x 15 in; 60 x 40 cm; 35 x 23 in; 90 x 60 cm
Image also used: Fundación Juan March,
Madrid, 1993
Detail from *Montcalm Interior With Two Dogs*, 1988

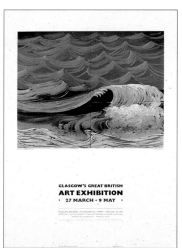

196 GLASGOW'S GREAT BRITISH ART
EXHIBITION

McLellan Galleries,1990
28 x 20 in; 70.9 x 50.6 cm
A Bigger Wave, 1989

197 DAVID HOCKNEY

Hancock Street, West Hollywood, 1989
36 x 24 in; 91.4 x 61 cm
Hancock Street, West Hollywood, 1989

198 DAVID HOCKNEY: SOME VERY
NEW PAINTINGS

1853 Gallery, Salts Mill, Bradford
24 x 39 in; 63 x 101 cm
The Other Side, 1990-93

199 CHELSEA ARTS BALL, 1992

Royal Albert Hall
23 x 14 in; 59.4 x 39.4 cm
Exuberant Arch, 1991

200 TURANDOT

San Francisco Opera, 1993
24 x 41 in; 61 x 104 cm
Computer laser generated print of Act I, 1991

201 TURANDOT

Lyric Opera of Chicago, 1992
36 x 10 in ; 91.5 x 26 cm
Computer laser generated print of Act II, 1991

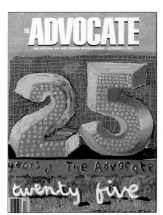

202 25 YEARS OF THE ADVOCATE

Based on the cover artwork of 'The Advocate',
1992
32 x 23 in; 83.3 x 60 cm
25 Years of 'The Advocate', 1992

203 DIE FRAU OHNE SCHATTEN

Los Angeles Music Center Opera 1993
30 x 20 in; 76 x 51.9 cm
Detail from The Golden River, 1992-3

204 DIE FRAU OHNE SCHATTEN

Royal Opera House, Covent Garden, 1992
30 x 22 in; 76 x 56 cm
Two versions produced
Untitled computer laser generated print in acrylic, 1992

205 FOR TIVOLI GARDENS 1993

Two posters made: 23 x 17 in; 60.4 x 43.7 cm,
34 x 25 in; 88.4 x 63.3 cm
Details from The Twenty Fourth VN Painting,
1992

206 DAVID HOCKNEY: SOME VERY
NEW PAINTINGS

William Hardie Gallery, Glasgow, 1993
16 x 11 in; 42 x 29.7 cm
The Eleventh VN Painting, 1992

207 SOME LOCAL SNAPS BY
DAVID HOCKNEY 1993

A Local Artist at 1853 Gallery, Salts Mill,
Bradford
33 x 22 in; 83.4 x 56.4 cm
Untitled, 1993